D1664533

Questions for *Christian* Couples Journal

Questions for *Christian* Couples

JOURNAL

365 Daily Questions to Grow
Closer to God and Each Other

EMILY JORDAN

**ROCKRIDGE
PRESS**

Unless otherwise indicated, all Scripture quotations are taken from the Holy Bible, New International Version®, NIV®. Copyright © 1973, 1978, 1984, 2011 by Biblica Inc.® Used by permission. All rights reserved worldwide. Scripture quotations marked (ESV) are taken from The Holy Bible, English Standard Version, copyright © 2001 by Crossway Bibles, a division of Good News Publishers. Used by permission. All rights reserved. Scripture quotations marked (NLT) are taken from the Holy Bible, New Living Translation, copyright © 1996, 2004, 2014 by Tyndale House Foundation. Used by permission of Tyndale House Publishers, Inc., Carol Stream, Illinois 60188. All rights reserved. Scripture quotations marked (KJV) are taken from the King James Version of the Bible. Public domain. Scripture quotations marked (NKJV) are taken from the New King James Version®, copyright © 1982 by Thomas Nelson. Used by permission. All rights reserved. All other quoted material is in the public domain.

Copyright © 2022 by Rockridge Press

All rights reserved. No part of this publication may be reproduced, stored in a retrieval system, or transmitted in any form or by any means, electronic, mechanical, photocopying, recording, scanning, or otherwise without the prior written permission of the Publisher. Requests to the Publisher for permission should be addressed to the Permissions Department, Rockridge Press, 1955 Broadway, Suite 400, Oakland, CA 94612.

First Rockridge Press trade paperback edition 2022

Rockridge Press and the Rockridge Press logo are trademarks or registered trademarks of Callisto Media Inc. and/or its affiliates in the United States and other countries and may not be used without written permission.

For general information on our other products and services, please contact our Customer Care Department within the United States at (866) 744-2665, or outside the United States at (510) 253-0500.

Paperback ISBN: 978-1-68539-315-1

Manufactured in the United States of America

Interior and Cover Designer: Lisa Schreiber
Art Producer: Megan Baggott
Editor: Laura Cerrone, Adrian Potts
Production Editor: Cassie Gitkin
Production Manager: Martin Worthington

Illustrations used under license from Shutterstock, iStock Photo, Creative Market; Myriam Van Neste
Author photo courtesy of Anna Thielen Photography

10 9 8 7 6 5 4 3 2 1 0

This journal belongs to:

_____

Introduction

I AM THRILLED you are undertaking this fun and thought-provoking journey through the *Questions for Christian Couples Journal*. Whether you are dating, are newlyweds, are in a long-term relationship, or have been married for years, the questions in this journal are meant to be a tool for you and your partner to grow closer to each other and to God.

Before we start, I'd like to introduce myself: Emily Jordan. I am passionate about weaving together faith and relationships, both in my own marriage with my husband and as the founder of the ministry The Joyful Stepmom. Matt and I were married in 2005, when my stepson was a sweet five-year-old. Seeing a need for ministerial encouragement for my own blended family, and the requests for Christian support from others, I began the ministry in 2013 as a place for Christian stepmoms to pray together. We have grown to include local chapters. We feature a weekly Marriage Monday post to share resources. I have had the opportunity to serve on an advisory board, speak at virtual conferences, and be a contributing writer on family and relationship resources.

I am also a lover and shameless collector of journals. Asking questions is a great way to explore and expand our relationships. When our son was young, we would play a game called Would You Rather, as in, "Would you rather have superstrength or x-ray vision?" The silly questions led to lots of laughs and further conversation.

Journals are a great tool for sharing thoughts and building dreams. During our time dating, my husband and I lived a little distance from each other. Between in-person visits, we spent a lot of time on the phone and corresponding over email to get to know one another. From those early days and into our marriage, I have journaled prayer time and processed our story. Writing is a wonderful way to share your thoughts and learn about your partner.

I have created this journal with 365 questions to read and discuss with your partner. The content is geared specifically to Christian couples who want to grow in connection and strengthen their relationship. As you both work your way through this journal, I hope you share, laugh, and grow in faith together. Enjoy the year ahead!

How to Use This Book

IN THIS JOURNAL, you'll find a question for each day of the year. Some are based on Bible verses and some are much broader. These questions are meant to spark thoughtful, fun, and faith-based conversations with your partner.

There is space under each question to record your responses. You can take turns writing, or you can use separate notebooks for your answers and then compare. You could also jot down a few thoughts using different pen colors, so your replies are recorded together. Have fun with it! Read, respond, and share your thoughts daily.

The 365 questions you'll find fall loosely into these four categories:

 Future goals/dreams

 Romantic/playful

 Past/present

 Philosophical/psychological

Start at the beginning of the journal and work your way through the year. Take a few moments each day to review the question before journaling your response. Share your responses with each other, and be intentional to listen and engage.

Now let's get started!

1 DATE: _____

First impressions can leave a lasting mark. It can be fun to hear what your partner first thought of you. Share your first impressions of meeting each other.

_____

_____

_____

_____

_____

_____

2 DATE: _____

You and your partner are at a coffee shop and someone from the Bible asks to sit at your table. Who is it and what would you like to talk about?

_____

_____

_____

_____

_____

_____

_____

3 DATE:_____

Ecclesiastes 4:12 refers to our greater strength in Christ: "Three are even better, for a triple-braided cord is not easily broken." (NLT) How are you intentionally bringing Christ into your relationship?

_____

_____

_____

_____

_____

4 DATE:_____

A mission statement summarizes an organization's values and ambitions. Write a mission statement for your relationship. What ambitions, goals, and spiritual values do you hold for your relationship?

_____

_____

_____

_____

_____

_____

5 DATE: _____

Prayer is our conversation with God. Do you and your partner pray together, or is it something you would like to introduce? What does this practice look like in your home?

_____

_____

_____

_____

_____

pray

6 DATE: _____

Imagine you've inherited one million dollars from a relative. The will stipulates that you must share and spend the money with your partner. How would you spend the inheritance together?

_____

_____

_____

_____

_____

_____

7 DATE: _____

Micah 6:8 teaches us "to do what is right, to love mercy, and to walk humbly with your God." (NLT) What causes or issues do you both champion passionately?

_____

_____

_____

_____

_____

_____

8 DATE: _____

On your next free, no-obligation weekend, how will you spend the time together? What plans would you like to make for fun, rest, or maybe a quick getaway?

_____

_____

_____

_____

_____

_____

_____

9 DATE: _____

In Colossians 3:14 Paul writes, "Above all, clothe your-selves with love, which binds us all together in perfect harmony." (NLT) How does your partner love you well?

_____

_____

_____   *blessed*

_____   *loved*

_____

_____

_____

10 DATE: _____

If you had the opportunity to work or serve in another country, would you leap at the chance? Where would you hope this opportunity would take you?

_____

_____

_____

_____

_____

_____

_____

11 DATE: _____

Do you have a person in your life who greatly affected your faith journey? Have you shared that story or intro- duced that person to your partner? Write about them here as a starting point for a conversation.

_____

_____

_____

_____

_____

_____

12 DATE: _____

Plan a future road trip. Where would you like to go together? And the ultimate question: Who is driving, and who will navigate and be in charge of snacks?

_____

_____

_____

_____

_____

_____

_____

_____

13 DATE: _____

Sharing our thoughts on faith brings us closer. Colossians 2:7 says, "Let your roots grow down into him." (NLT) What is a spiritual topic you'd like to explore with your partner?

_____

_____

_____

_____

_____

_____

_____

14 DATE: _____

You and your partner are out shopping and enter a sporting goods store. Which section do you each go to first? Is there a shared interest or a new hobby you can try together?

_____

_____

_____

_____

_____

_____

15 DATE: _____

Think about an experience where you felt like the under-dog but ended up being triumphant. Celebrate and describe the emotion of realizing your full potential.

_____

_____

_____

_____

_____

_____

_____

Stay
STRONG
→»→→→

16 DATE: _____

Some of us have big plans for retirement and others are reveling in that season now. What are your retirement goals? If you're already there, are you living the way you had dreamed?

_____

_____

_____

_____

_____

_____

_____

17 DATE: _____

We rejoice in Psalm 139:14: "Thank you for making me so wonderfully complex!" (NLT) Although you were created uniquely, do you and your partner share certain traits? How do you find a balance?

_____

_____

_____

_____

_____

_____

18 DATE: _____

People sometimes refer to their "happy place"—a physical or mental place of rest and relaxation. Where is your shared happy place where you find renewal together?

_____

_____

_____

_____

_____

_____

19 DATE: _____

At some time during your relationship, you will face loss. Share how you have supported each other and what you appreciated about your partner during that season—or how you will support each other during such a season in the future.

_____

_____

_____

_____

_____

_____

20 DATE: _____

Imagine you have the opportunity to build your dream house together. What features will it have? Would you build in an urban, suburban, or rural area? Any particular location?

_____

_____

_____

_____

_____

_____

_____

21 DATE: _____

Our backgrounds shape us. As you build a life together, how will you be able to blend your different spiritual backgrounds, set values for your home, or choose a place of worship?

_____

_____

_____

_____

_____

_____

_____

22 DATE: _____

Reminisce about your first date. Now plan a reenactment— with a twist! How would you update your plans for that first date to reflect who you are today as a couple?

_____

_____

_____

_____

_____

_____

_____

23 DATE: _____

In Jeremiah 29:11 the Lord says, "For I know the plans I have for you." When you were children, what did you each hope to be when you grew up? How has the Lord directed your steps toward or away from that dream?

_____

_____

_____

_____

_____

_____

24 DATE: _____

Where do you see yourselves as a couple in 10 years? What are some specific steps you can take to move in that direction?

_____

_____

_____

_____

_____

_____

_____

25 DATE: _____

In Psalm 104:19 we learn that seasonal changes are a purposeful part of creation: "He made the moon to mark the seasons." What are your favorite seasons and why?

_____

_____

_____

_____

_____

_____

_____

26 DATE: _____

We can get so caught up in day-to-day activities that we forget to voice what we love about each other. Take a moment to write down and share your partner's best character traits and qualities.

_____

_____

_____

_____

_____

_____

_____

27 DATE: _____

Share a time of disappointment. How were you able to cope together?

_____

_____

_____

_____

_____

_____

_____

Faith

28 DATE: _____

Relationships need maintenance care. How can you intentionally build love into your relationship through resources like retreats, books, or journals? Make a plan to use more resources like this one.

_____

_____

_____

_____

_____

_____

_____

29 DATE: _____

1 Corinthians 12:8 teaches us that spiritual gifts are "given to each of us so we can help each other." (NLT) What are your spiritual gifts and how do you use them to help each other?

_____

_____

_____

_____

_____

_____

30 DATE: _____

It's spring break and you two are going on a trip. Are you going to the mountains to hike, the beach to relax, or an amusement park for some excitement?

_____

_____

_____

_____

_____

_____

_____

31 DATE: _____

Is there a place that holds great meaning for you as a couple? Write about it and share with your partner.

_____

_____

_____

_____

_____

_____

_____

32 DATE: _____

Is there a shared activity you both enjoy but have not done recently? What holds you back? What steps can you take to return to it?

_____

_____

_____

_____

_____

_____

_____

33 DATE: _____

Throughout the Bible we see people turn to their elders for wisdom. Do you have a mentor couple you are both comfortable seeking out for help in your relationship?

_____

_____

_____

_____

_____

_____

34 DATE: _____

It's game night! What games will you be playing together? Can you guess which game your partner will pick and explain why they love that choice?

_____

_____

_____

_____

_____

_____

_____

35 DATE: _____

In Philemon 1:6 Paul writes, "I am praying you will put into action the generosity that comes from your faith." (NLT) Have you ever been wildly generous? How did it feel?

_____

_____

_____

_____

_____

_____

_____

36 DATE: _____

Is there a subject you talk about on replay together? For example, taking a certain trip, planting a garden, or adopting a pet. Discuss steps you could take toward realizing that dream.

_____

_____

_____

_____

_____

_____

37 DATE: _____

In Psalm 119:11 David writes, "I have hidden your word in my heart." Do you spend time reading the Bible together? How does this spiritual time together enhance your relationship?

_____

_____

_____

_____

_____

_____

38 DATE: _____

It's fun to work together in the kitchen. If your partner were a famous chef, who do you think they would be and why? What dish do they make as a family favorite?

_____

_____

_____

_____

_____

_____

_____

39 DATE: _____

How have you communicated about major purchases in the past? How can you improve communication in this area when new needs arise?

_____

_____

_____

_____

_____

_____

_____

40 DATE: _____

It's healthy to build and maintain our personal friendships. How do you value individual friendships and still respect your relationship time?

_____

_____

_____

_____

_____

_____

41 DATE: _____

Reaching goals is more fun with a partner to encourage and cheer us toward victory. Do you have any healthy lifestyle goals that you are working toward together?

_____

_____

_____

_____

_____

_____

_____

42 DATE: _____

Are you a rule-follower or more lax about guidelines? What about your partner? How do you balance each other?

_____

_____

_____

_____

_____

_____

43 DATE: _____

If you spent a week living off the grid, what would be your most difficult tech resource to give up? Do you think your partner would enjoy the week?

_____

_____

_____

_____

_____

_____

44 DATE: _____

Giving your time is a great thing to do together. Do you serve in the same area of church or community? Is this an area you would like to explore?

_____

_____

_____

_____

_____

_____

45 DATE: _____

Proverbs 27:17 says, "As iron sharpens iron, so one person sharpens another." While being a couple, though, you can also pursue your own passions. How do you encourage each other to pursue individual goals?

_____

_____

_____

_____

_____

_____

46 DATE: _____

Settling into schedules and patterns can be a learning curve as you get to know each other. Are you early risers or night owls? How do make space for each other's needs?

_____

_____

_____

_____

_____

_____

47 DATE: _____

In Matthew 28:20 Jesus said, "I am with you always."
Write about a time you felt the Lord's presence either
through prayer or tangible provision. Share this sacred
moment with your partner.

_____

_____

_____

_____

_____

_____

_____

48 DATE: _____

How would you like to celebrate a major milestone in your
relationship—perhaps an anniversary, a commitment met,
or a goal reached? Make plans to honor that achievement.

_____

_____

_____

_____

_____

_____

49 DATE: _____

As part of your faith journey, you may choose a life verse from the Bible. Share your verse and the reason you like it. Perhaps this is a good time to choose one.

_____

_____

_____

_____

_____

_____

_____

50 DATE: _____

Let's go to the amusement park! Where are you both headed first? To the tallest roller coaster, for a funnel cake, or are you people-watching on a bench?

_____

_____

_____

_____

_____

_____

_____

51 DATE: _____

You can learn a lot about what people value by asking, "If we had to evacuate right now, what three things would you grab?" Any surprising answers between you?

_____

_____

_____

_____

_____

_____

_____

52 DATE: _____

What unique anniversaries (not your wedding) or dates on the calendar do you celebrate, and how do you observe these days? What do you have planned for your next special occasion together?

_____

_____

_____

_____

_____

_____

53 DATE: _____

Colossians 3:16 says, "Let the message about Christ, in all its richness, fill your lives." (NLT) How has memorizing a Bible verse had an impact for you? Can you memorize a verse together?

_____

_____

_____

_____

_____

_____

54 DATE: _____

We are going to the bookstore! You both enter and grab a coffee together. Now which subject area of the store are you going to first? Will you browse together?

_____

_____

_____

_____

_____

_____

55 DATE: _____

Often, we divide household chores between us, either by skill or just by who's available. Who's making dinner tonight? How do you divide daily tasks?

_____

_____

_____

_____

_____

_____

56 DATE: _____

The greatest thing you can do for someone is pray. How precious to be able to pray for your partner! Do you have a specific prayer request to share with each other?

_____

_____

_____

_____

_____

_____

57 DATE: _____

Our legacy is what we leave behind—the memories and impact we share with others. What do you think your legacy will be? How do you hope to be remembered?

_____

_____

_____

_____

_____

_____

_____

58 DATE: _____

Which one of you is in charge of the playlist in the car? Do you tune in to podcasts or music? What's your favorite genre to listen to when you drive together?

_____

_____

_____

_____

_____

_____

_____

59 DATE: _____

We hear the cry of David in Psalm 38:15: "For I am waiting for you, O Lord." (NLT) Have you been in a season of waiting? How did you encourage each other?

_____

_____

_____

_____

_____

_____

_____

60 DATE: _____

Building a community of friendships is a great gift, but it can be difficult at times. How can you build community with other couples, through your church, or elsewhere?

_____

_____

_____

_____

_____

_____

_____

61 DATE: _____

Matthew 20:16 reminds us, "The last shall be first, and the first, last." (KJV) In what areas do you put your partner first? How does that make you feel?

_____

_____

_____

_____

_____

_____

62 DATE: _____

It's a snowy winter day. Where are you two? Cuddled by the fire with hot cocoa or out skiing? What is your ideal winter day together?

_____

_____

_____

_____

_____

_____

love

63 DATE: _____

God has called us to be peacemakers. What have you done well to maintain peace in your home and relationship? What can you work on to improve in this area?

_____

_____

_____

_____

_____

_____

64 DATE: _____

What are your career goals for the next five years? Are you interested in a change or are you happy with your current work?

_____

_____

_____

_____

_____

_____

65 DATE: _____

Sometimes we say, "It's been a tough year, but we made it. What a blessing!" How would you describe your greatest blessing so far in your relationship? What has made all the difference?

_____

_____

_____

_____

_____

_____   *Blessed*

_____

66 DATE: _____

It's a typical quiet evening after dinner and you want to watch a show together. What do you choose? Is it a comedy, a mystery, or maybe a drama?

_____

_____

_____

_____

_____

_____

67 DATE: _____

In 2 Samuel 6:5, David and the people of Israel are "celebrating with all their might before God, with songs and with harps." What is your worship style?

_____

_____

_____

_____

_____

_____

_____

68 DATE: _____

The two of you are taking a walk on the beach and stumble upon a wedding in progress. Do you back away quietly, stop to watch, or carry on with your walk? Why?

_____

_____

_____

_____

_____

_____

_____

69 DATE: _____

Luke 13:29 describes heaven as a "feast in the kingdom of God." Through our faith, we develop a vision of heaven. What do you think heaven will be like?

_____

_____

_____

_____

_____

_____

70 DATE: _____

Do either of you have a green thumb? If you had a garden space to share, what would you plant there? Would it thrive?

_____

_____

_____

_____

_____

_____

71 DATE: _____

We all get struck by jealousy from time to time. How do you handle this emotion in your relationship? How can you help each other work through it and feel secure?

_____

_____

_____

_____

_____

_____

72 DATE: _____

Is there an area where you have watched your partner struggle? What is some encouragement you can share with them? How have you seen them work toward a triumph?

_____

_____

_____

_____

_____

_____

Hope

73 DATE: _____

Just as we age physically, we grow and age spiritually. How has your faith changed and developed over the years? How has that affected your life choices?

_____

_____

_____

_____

_____

_____

_____

74 DATE: _____

Imagine you are the host of a podcast about relationships. Who would you invite on as a guest and what kind of relationship advice would seek from them?

_____

_____

_____

_____

_____

_____

_____

75 DATE: _____

In 1 Thessalonians 5:16 Paul writes, "Always be joyful." (NLT)
How do you show your joy for your partner? What is a
tangible way you can express your joy in each other?

_____

_____

_____

_____

_____

_____   *Joyful*

_____

76 DATE: _____

Preparation can take the power out of something, such as
fear. What is something you fear? How can you prepare
for it to minimize the burden on your heart?

_____

_____

_____

_____

_____

_____

_____

77 DATE: _____

Psalm 23 begins with David writing, "The Lord is my shepherd." What are three words you would use to describe your relationship with God in this season of your faith?

_____

_____

_____

_____

_____

78 DATE: _____

Picture the president calling and requesting your help with a national crisis. Only your superpowers can save the world from impending disaster. What superpower do you each have?

_____

_____

_____

_____

_____

_____

_____

79 DATE: _____

We are often separated from each other during the day. What is your lunch routine? Share who is at your table and what is usually on the menu as a way to learn about each other's day.

_____

_____

_____

_____

_____

80 DATE: _____

Let's say you need to have a difficult conversation with a friend or coworker. You want a positive outcome! Where would you start? Write about it, then brainstorm with your partner.

_____

_____

_____

_____

_____

81 DATE: _____

The spiritual definition of grace is the free or unmerited favor God gives, or we can give, to a person. How are you able to show grace to your partner?

_____

_____

_____

_____

_____

_____

_____

82 DATE: _____

A quaint historic town has a storefront opening available and the two of you have decided to rent the space. What kind of shop would you open together?

_____

_____

_____

_____

_____

_____

_____

83 DATE: _____

Name a favorite book or movie that you can return to again and again without growing weary. What is it that draws you to this particular story?

_____

_____

_____

_____

_____

_____

_____

84 DATE: _____

Weekends are often a time for the to-do list. Is there a home-improvement project you've been meaning to tackle? What is the first step you can take together toward making it happen?

_____

_____

_____

_____

_____

_____

_____

85 DATE: _____

Some people see the glass as half empty, others know it to be half full. Are you and your loved one optimists or pessimists, and how do you balance each other?

_____

_____

_____

_____

_____

_____

86 DATE: _____

Time to head out to sea! If you took a cruise, where would you like to go? What would you consider to be a vital item to bring on the voyage?

_____

_____

_____

_____

_____

_____

87 DATE: _____

An older home is sometimes described as having good bones. It means the infrastructure is solid and of good quality. What qualities would you describe as the good bones of your relationship?

_____

_____

_____

_____

_____

_____

88 DATE: _____

In Matthew 5:44 the Apostle teaches us to "love your enemies! Pray for those who persecute you!" Is there someone in your life you should be praying for?

_____

_____

_____

_____

_____

_____

 **89** DATE: _____

We can get stuck in a rut with our meals. What is a new dish you'd like to try making together this week? Why does it pique your interest?

_____

_____

_____

_____

_____

_____

90 DATE: _____

The Apostle Paul writes in Colossians 3:13, "Remember, the Lord forgave you, so you must forgive others." (NLT) How have you been able to show forgiveness to your partner?

_____

_____

_____

_____

_____

_____

_____

91 DATE: _____

Often we look to our family roots for the beginnings of building our own family. What is a favorite family tradition that you carry on in your own home?

_____

_____

_____

_____

_____

_____

_____

92 DATE: _____

We feel close and build our relationship when we communicate. Reminding your partner of what you love about them builds strength. What are three things you love about each other?

_____

_____

_____

_____

_____

_____

93 DATE: _____

How do you view the current atmosphere or mood in your home? What can you do together to make it feel more inviting?

_____

_____

_____

_____

_____

_____

94 DATE: _____

Take a moment to write separately from your partner. Describe your perfect day together. Now come back together and compare notes. See what kind of amazing adventure you can plan!

_____

_____

_____

_____

_____

_____

_____

95 DATE: _____

In Ephesians 4:2 Paul writes, "Always be humble and gentle." We often are admonished to be kind or patient with each other. How can you be gentle with your loved one?

_____

_____

_____

_____

_____

_____

96 DATE: _____

We are bound to hurt each other—we're only human. It's how we handle the hurt that counts. Apologizing is difficult, but important. Is there anything you need to apologize for?

_____

_____

_____

_____

_____   *keep no*

_____   *record of*

_____   *wrongs*

97 DATE: _____

They say beauty is in the eye of the beholder. Do you enjoy the same styles and media of art? Share your favorite artist or a sample of their work.

_____

_____

_____

_____

_____

_____

_____

98 DATE: _____

Whether you have been together 50 days or 50 years, romance is important in every relationship. What is a grand romantic gesture your loved one has done for you?

_____

_____

_____

_____

_____

_____

_____

99 DATE: _____

What is something you used to do together that has slipped through the cracks over time? How can you bring that back into your lives?

_____

_____

_____

_____

_____

_____

_____

100 DATE: _____

James 1:5 says, "If you need wisdom, ask our generous God." (NLT) We can ask God anything. When you get to heaven, what is the first thing you want to ask?

_____

_____

_____

_____

_____

_____

_____

101 DATE: _____

We often begin our love with attraction, before growing closer. If you had to significantly alter your appearance, how would your partner react to that change?

_____

_____

_____

_____

_____

_____

102 DATE: _____

What is a hobby you really enjoyed as a child? Would you like to pick it up again as an adult or share it with your own children someday?

_____

_____

_____

_____

_____

_____

pray

103 DATE: _____

The Bible leaves a legacy of faith for us to learn and grow. Is there a particular person's story in the Bible that has had an impact on your spiritual journey?

_____

_____

_____

_____

_____

_____

104 DATE: _____

Estate planning is a heavy financial topic many people put off. But if you dream big, what kind of financial legacy would you love to leave your family or a charity?

_____

_____

_____

_____

_____

_____

_____

105 DATE: _____

A common phrase of encouragement is, "God will never give you more than you can handle." How do you feel about that? Does it feel true and encouraging to you?

_____

_____

_____

_____

_____

_____ TRUST

_____

106 DATE: _____

If you could only eat one thing for the rest of your life, what would it be? Would you lean toward sweet, salty, sour, maybe some carbs?

_____

_____

_____

_____

_____

_____

_____

107 DATE: _____

Share a part of your history with your loved one. How does this background make you who you are today?

_____

_____

_____

_____

_____

_____

_____

trusts

108 DATE: _____

We all have personal and/or professional dreams, and it takes hard work to bring them to life. What is a sacrifice you have made for a family or career goal?

_____

_____

_____

_____

_____

_____

_____

109 DATE: _____

If someone came to you seeking to grow in the Lord or asking questions about a relationship with God, how would you describe the impact faith has had on your life?

_____

_____

_____

_____

_____

_____

110 DATE: _____

Imagine you have a budget of twenty dollars for date night. What would you plan for a date together? How creative can you be with this budget?

_____

_____

_____

_____

_____

_____

111 DATE: _____

We want our family and close friends to share in the joy of our love. How did you introduce your significant other to your family and friends, and how was the experience?

_____

_____

_____

_____

_____

_____

112 DATE: _____

We can all become a little complacent and take our favorite people for granted. Have you done that with your partner? If so, how can you move your relationship to a place of priority in your life?

_____

_____

_____

_____

_____

_____

LOVE

113 DATE: _____

It is a difficult subject many of us face at some point in our spiritual journey. How do you answer the question, "Why does God let bad things happen?"

_____

_____

_____

_____

_____

_____

_____

114 DATE: _____

Have you ever had the opportunity to ride in a hot air balloon? If you had the opportunity, would you do it? Tell your partner why that sounds exciting—or why it doesn't.

_____

_____

_____

_____

_____

_____

_____

115 DATE: _____

How often are you able to sit down and have dinner together? What would you like to improve about that routine? Do you sit at the table and pray together first?

_____

_____

_____

_____

_____

_____

3 ♥ 16

116 DATE: _____

How can you plan to care for each other during a health crisis? What brings you comfort when you feel under the weather?

_____

_____

_____

_____

_____

_____

117 DATE: _____

Do you verbally share your faith or do you prefer to let your actions speak for themselves? John 13:35 says, "Your love for one another will prove to the world that you are my disciples."

_____

_____

_____

_____

_____

_____

_____

118 DATE: _____

You have decided to adopt a pet together. What kind of animal will you be looking for? And the most important question: What is the pet's name?

_____

_____

_____

_____

_____

_____

_____

 **119** DATE: _____

When faced with a difficult situation in your past, how did that situation change you as a person? Did it affect your view of relationships or change your goals?

_____

_____

_____

_____

_____

_____

120 DATE: _____

Write about and share with your partner a personal or professional goal you have been working toward this year. What steps have you taken to achieve that dream? How can they help?

_____

_____

_____

_____

_____

_____ HOPE

_____

121 DATE: _____

In 1 Chronicles 16:24 Ezra writes, "Publish his glorious deeds among the nations." (NLT) It is an encouragement to share praise and a grateful heart. What are you grateful for today?

_____

_____

_____

_____

_____   *grateful*

_____

122 DATE: _____

Exercise is important and something we can share with our partner. Would you rather run a marathon, take the dog for a walk, do yoga (on the floor or in a chair), or do some stretching together?

_____

_____

_____

_____

_____

_____

123 DATE: _____

Our family roots and traditions have sentimental value to us. Is there a lost family heirloom you wish you still had? What made it so special to you and your family?

_____

_____

_____

_____

_____

_____

124 DATE: _____

When opportunity knocks, it's tempting to accept any and all openings. How do you prioritize a good opportunity and still keep a balance for family time?

_____

_____

_____

_____

_____

_____

_____

125 DATE: _____

John 16:33 says, "You will have many trials and sorrows. But take heart, because I have overcome the world." (NLT) How has faith helped you through a difficult season in your relationship?

_____

_____

_____

_____

_____

_____ Faith

_____

126 DATE: _____

It's pizza night! A question that can stump the most devoted couples: Where are you ordering your pizza from—or is it homemade? What are your pizza toppings?

_____

_____

_____

_____

_____

_____

_____

127 DATE: _____

Scent can be very soothing or remind us of a place or person from our past. What is your favorite scent and what does that smell remind you of?

_____

_____

_____

_____

_____

_____

_____

128 DATE: _____

Sometimes it's all about the little things between us. What small acts of kindness or words of encouragement can you start offering each other regularly?

_____

_____

_____

_____

_____

_____

_____

129 DATE: _____

In 1 Peter 1:7, the Apostle writes of our faith, "It is being tested as fire tests and purifies gold." (NLT) How has your faith been tested by a refining fire?

_____

_____

_____

_____

_____

_____

130 DATE: _____

Date night can be as elaborate as dinner and a show or as simple as ice cream and a walk in the park. Do you typically have a regularly scheduled date night or a spontaneous night out? Would you spend more special time together if you planned for it?

_____

_____

_____

_____

_____

**131** DATE: _____

Who was your favorite teacher in school and what qualities made them so memorable? Was it something academic, something about their personality, or the things they did that you admired?

_____

_____

_____

_____

_____

_____

_____

132 DATE: _____

What is something no one would ever expect you to do—maybe even a surprise to yourself—that you would be proud or excited to accomplish someday?

_____

_____

_____

_____

_____

_____

133 DATE: _____

When we're in a relationship, we can become caught up in the togetherness of it all. How do you work to give each other personal time and space inside your relationship?

_____

_____

_____

_____

_____

_____

_____

134 DATE: _____

What is your favorite holiday or celebration? Why do you enjoy that celebration best? Do you prefer a large social gathering or a more intimate setting? What about traveling versus staying home?

_____

_____

_____

_____

_____

_____

_____

135 DATE: _____

Hebrews 6:15 says, "Abraham waited patiently, and he received what God had promised." (NLT) What is something you have asked of the Lord and the response was that you need to wait?

_____

_____

_____

_____

_____   *patient*

_____

136 DATE: _____

1 Corinthians 12:25 urges us "that there may be no division in the body, but that the members may have the same care for one another." (ESV) What is one thing you wish your community had and what can you do to help make it a reality?

_____

_____

_____

_____

_____

_____

137 DATE: _____

Isaiah 41:13 says, "Do not fear; I will help you." How have you handled seasons of self-doubt? What can you do to support and encourage your partner?

_____

_____

_____

_____

_____

_____

138 DATE: _____

Music has been called the language of love for its emotional connection. What was your first concert and who would you love to see in a live performance?

_____

_____

_____

_____

_____

_____

_____

139 DATE: _____

Write about and share an accomplishment of yours that you wish your partner could have witnessed and celebrated with you. What would you like them to know about that special triumph?

_____

_____

_____

_____

_____

_____

140 DATE: _____

If a close friend or family member needed your assistance, how would you plan to help? What are ways you could both agree to assist them?

_____

_____

_____

_____

_____ *GRACE*

141 DATE: _____

Imagine you have been entrusted with secret or confidential information. Will you share that information with your partner? What conditions might change your answer and your reasoning?

_____

_____

_____

_____

_____

_____

_____

142 DATE: _____

You are attending a class and have been assigned to write an essay about something you know a lot about. What is your topic, and how can you collaborate with your partner?

_____

_____

_____

_____

_____

_____

143 DATE: _____

Many people would say age is just a number. How has the age difference or proximity with your partner enhanced your relationship and made it stronger?

_____

_____

_____

_____

_____

_____

_____

144 DATE: _____

King Solomon writes in Proverbs 27:9, "The heartfelt counsel of a friend is as sweet as perfume." (NLT) What qualities do you look for and value in a friendship?

_____

_____

_____

_____

_____

_____

_____

145 DATE: _____

Would you consider yourself to be a good listener? Can
you think of a situation in which the act of listening made
all the difference in the outcome?

_____

_____

_____

_____

_____

_____

146 DATE: _____

A little competition is fun between partners. What are the
two of you most competitive about? Do you feel you keep
the game at a healthy level?

_____

_____

_____

_____

_____

_____

147 DATE: _____

The Bible speaks repeatedly about taking a Sabbath day of rest. How can you reserve space in your schedule, mentally and spiritually, for a time of rest and renewal?

_____

_____

_____

_____

_____

_____

148 DATE: _____

Relationships are about give and take, sharing the burden together. What is something you can do for your partner to ease their burden, either with home chores or mental stressors?

_____

_____

_____

_____

_____   *Peace*

_____

149 DATE: _____

Matthew 5:25 speaks about anger saying, "settle matters quickly." Conflict will happen, but how are the two of you able to make amends and resolve the conflict quickly?

_____

_____

_____

_____

_____

_____

_____

GRACE

150 DATE: _____

The car has been making a funny screeching noise this week. Are you more inclined to make an appointment at the auto shop or pop the hood and fix it yourself?

_____

_____

_____

_____

_____

_____

_____

151 DATE: _____

What do you think is the secret glue that holds couples together for many, many years? What qualities of their relationship are the keys to longevity?

_____

_____

_____

_____

_____

_____

152 DATE: _____

How comfortable are you with big life changes? Do you embrace the impending shifts in your life or do they cause anxiety? How can your partner help you handle the adjustment?

_____

_____

_____

_____

_____

_____

153 DATE:_____

Throughout the Bible we see prayers of thanksgiving.
Write a prayer of thanksgiving to share with your partner
and reflect on incorporating this into your prayer routine.

_____

_____

_____

_____

_____

_____

154 DATE:_____

Something ominous goes bump in the dark of night.
Which of you is more likely to get up and investigate?
Which of you will be hiding under the covers?

_____

_____

_____

_____

_____

_____

155 DATE: _____

When the alarm clock rings, some of us are up and out the door while others wake up more slowly. Share your morning routine and habits with your significant other.

_____

_____

_____

_____

_____

_____

156 DATE: _____

Sometimes, as couples, we lose track of our friendships because of the busyness of family, work, and life. Who is a friend you want to stay close with through it all?

_____

_____

_____

_____

_____

_____

157 DATE: _____

Can you put a time limit on God answering your prayers? Is it ever acceptable to pray and ask the Lord for an answer within a certain timeframe?

_____

_____

_____

_____

_____

_____

_____

158 DATE: _____

How is your internal navigation system wired? Can you point to the north? Try writing out how to get from work or your friend's house to your home using east and west directions.

_____

_____

_____

_____

_____

_____

_____

159 DATE: _____

Between birthdays, holidays, and anniversaries, what is the best present you have ever received from your partner? How did it speak to your heart and show their love?

_____

_____

_____

_____

_____

_____

_____

160 DATE: _____

If children are a part of your plan, what is a vacation or event you would like to experience with them? If children are not in your plan, is there a child-oriented thing you'd like to do with your partner?

_____

_____

_____

_____

_____

_____

161 DATE: _____

Scholars have long pondered the spirituality of children. Do you believe children, with their tender age and limited exposure to the world, are automatically brought into heaven after an untimely death?

_____

_____

_____

_____

_____

_____

162 DATE: _____

If Netflix made a movie about your relationship, what actors would you want to play you and your partner? What makes them the best fit to play your roles?

_____

_____

_____

_____

_____

_____

_____

163 DATE: _____

Do you belong to a church? If so, what ministries were you looking for when you chose your church? Maybe a youth ministry, a choir, or a specific support group?

_____

_____

_____

_____

_____

_____

164 DATE: _____

You will be faced with making big decisions together as a couple. What is your process for making big decisions as a team? How are you understanding of each other?

_____

_____

_____

_____

_____

_____

165 DATE: _____

Topics of faith will occasionally come up in conversations with friends or coworkers. How can you gently share your faith and be a good listener?

_____

_____

_____

_____

_____

_____

166 DATE: _____

If you could buy any car for you and your partner, what would it be? Imagine cost is no object. What features and what color would you choose?

_____

_____

_____

_____

_____

_____

_____

167 DATE: _____

It's spring and the yard needs work (or maybe the terrace or the plants on the windowsill). Imagine you can be completely creative with your natural space. What would you design and why? There are no financial constraints, so get creative!

_____

_____

_____

_____

_____

168 DATE: _____

Now that we are in the age of space tourism, would you go to space for vacation? How do you imagine the experience?

_____

_____

_____

_____

_____

_____

_____

169 DATE: _____

Write about where you are now in your spiritual journey. Are you feeling growth and wanting to dig deeper? Or are you in a place of listening and seeking?

_____

_____

_____

_____

_____

_____

170 DATE: _____

If you could convince your partner to try one food or meal that they might not have considered or have refused in the past, what would it be and why?

_____

_____

_____

_____

_____

_____

_____

171 DATE: _____

If you had the opportunity to switch careers and do something radically different for one year before returning to your current job, would you jump at the chance? Why or why not?

_____

_____

_____

_____

_____

_____

_____

172 DATE: _____

For your next milestone birthday, how would you like to be celebrated? Share some thoughts and give some hints to your partner for their plans to honor you.

_____

_____

_____

_____

_____

_____

_____

173 DATE: _____

We all hope to be an example to future generations. What qualities in your relationship do you most hope your children (or children who know you) will notice and emulate in their own relationships?

_____

_____

_____

_____

_____

_____

_____

174 DATE: _____

Romans 12:10 says, "Be devoted to one another in love." Feel good about being nice to each other! What is something you did for your partner that made you feel good?

_____

_____

_____

_____

_____

_____

_____

175 DATE: _____

Do you ever feel you would have been better suited to have lived in a different place and/or time period? What place and time would you have liked to experience?

_____

_____

_____

_____

_____

_____

176 DATE: _____

Trust is a foundational element of a loving relationship that stands the test of time. What can you do to build and strengthen the trust you have already established between you?

_____

_____

_____

_____

_____

_____

177 DATE: _____

What brings peace and calm to your emotions? Is it a quiet space, movement, or maybe music? Or do you find calm while being around people or nature?

_____

_____

_____

_____

_____

_____

_____

178 DATE: _____

An eccentric millionaire has buried their fortune and you are given three clues to its location. Would you try to find the treasure and what would be your strategy?

_____

_____

_____

_____

_____

_____

_____

179 DATE: _____

Past experiences can bring relationship fears into our hearts and cast a shadow over current love. What fears do you have about growing close to a loved one?

_____

_____

_____

_____

_____

Faith

180 DATE: _____

God planted a seed in your heart, a calling to your purpose or perhaps to a ministry. Have you embraced that calling? What might be holding you back, or how have you overcome obstacles?

_____

_____

_____

_____

_____

_____

_____

181 DATE: _____

Social media has become a popular form of communication and connection. How active are you on social media platforms and what do you enjoy or not enjoy about connecting in this way?

_____

_____

_____

_____

_____

_____

182 DATE: _____

You are going to a dinner party at a friend's house, and they ask you to bring a dish to share. What is your signature dish to pass and share?

_____

_____

_____

_____

_____

_____

183 DATE: _____

Consider a season of life when your strength of spirit was tested. How did the experience change you? Did it make you stronger or change your perspective on life?

_____

_____

_____

_____

_____

_____

184 DATE: _____

Have you fasted or removed something from your life to focus on God? Some Christians fast from food, media, or other things. Describe your experience or how you might like to incorporate something like this into your own faith journey.

_____

_____

_____

_____

_____

_____

_____

185 DATE: _____

When it's time to stand up for your convictions, how do you draw that boundary? How do you establish the line in the sand that you will not cross?

_____

_____

_____

_____

_____

_____

_____

186 DATE: _____

We all love a welcoming home, but what does that mean to you? What is your home decorating style, or what do you love about your living space?

_____

_____

_____

_____

_____

_____

_____

187 DATE: _____

When you are in crisis mode, who do you turn to for help
and support besides each other? How have they been a
support to you during a crisis?

_____

_____

_____

_____

_____

_____

188 DATE: _____

Matthew 2:13 tells us, "An angel of the Lord appeared to
Joseph in a dream. 'Get up,' he said, 'take the child and
his mother and escape to Egypt.'" Do you think God still
speaks to us through dreams?

_____

_____

_____

_____

_____

_____

_____

189 DATE: _____

Do you work well under pressure? When the deadline is looming and the minutes are ticking down, is this your time to shine or your time to panic?

_____

_____

_____

_____

_____

_____

190 DATE: _____

Imagine you are asked to write a coffee table book together. What would your subject be? These are usually visual books, so what kind of photography or artwork would you include?

_____

_____

_____

_____

_____

_____

191 DATE: _____

Easter has come to involve bunnies and egg hunts as well as Christ's sacrifice on the cross. How do you honor the holiday and how do you choose to celebrate?

_____

_____

_____

_____

_____

_____

192 DATE: _____

Feedback or constructive criticism can be a good way to help us improve our skills. How well do you accept feedback as a tool to improve and move forward with your goals?

_____

_____

_____

_____

_____

_____

193 DATE: _____

Trust typically means we have placed our faith or belief in someone or something. How can we grow in our trust of God? How can you encourage each other to trust in the Lord?

_____

_____

_____

_____

_____ TRUST

_____

194 DATE: _____

It's a night on the town! Are you lovebirds going to a five-star restaurant, a local diner, a tried-and-true favorite, or just for a stroll around town? What draws you to this place?

_____

_____

_____

_____

_____

_____

_____

195 DATE: _____

At work or at home, what keeps you both organized? What is your must-have tool or resource for staying on task and keeping life on track?

_____

_____

_____

_____

_____

_____

196 DATE: _____

How is your current relationship with your neighbors and those living around you? What can you do as a couple to improve those relationships and build community in your neighborhood?

_____

_____

_____

_____

_____

_____

197 DATE: _____

Write about a time you were brave in the face of fear, anxiety, or danger. Share the situation and your triumph with your partner.

_____

_____

_____

_____

_____

_____

_____

198 DATE: _____

What are your favorite TV shows or films that you connect with your faith? Do you both share any of the same ones?

_____

_____

_____

_____

_____

_____

_____

199 DATE: _____

Do you consider yourself to have healthy money habits?
What kind of spender are you? Do you tuck savings
away for a rainy day or enjoy the fruits of working hard
right away?

_____

_____

_____

_____

_____

200 DATE: _____

How would you describe your relationship to family? Perhaps you have friends that are adopted as family? How
can you nurture these relationships to include you as a
couple?

_____

_____

_____

_____

_____

_____

201 DATE: _____

What are you known for among friends, family, or colleagues? Would people talk about your humor, punctuality, or maybe your cooking skills? What do you want to be known for?

_____

_____

_____

_____

_____

_____

_____

202 DATE: _____

What kind of comedy makes you laugh? Are you more tickled by sarcasm or slapstick? Maybe you enjoy a good dad joke. What makes you laugh loudest?

_____

_____

_____

_____

_____

_____

203 DATE: _____

Much of the New Testament is composed of letters written to a town or to a dear friend. Do you still write letters or anything long form? Who do you send them to?

_____

_____

_____

_____

_____

_____

204 DATE: _____

Write for a few minutes about how you hope your future family will look. Are there children and grandchildren in your vision? Other kinds of family? Share these thoughts with each other.

_____

_____

_____

_____

_____

_____

_____

_____

205 DATE: _____

Do you believe God can use our stories of struggle and pain to teach others of His glory and healing? How has He done that with your life story?

_____

_____

_____

_____

_____

_____

206 DATE: _____

You are out on a date and it's open mic night with an impromptu talent show! What is your hidden talent and how will the two of you perform?

_____

_____

_____

_____

_____

_____

207 DATE: _____

Proverbs 4:25 says, "Let your eyes look straight ahead; fix your gaze directly before you." Forgiving the past, what present joy can you focus on together?

_____

_____

_____

_____

_____

_____

208 DATE: _____

What holidays do each of your families celebrate? How do you balance or navigate these special seasons? Is there a way you hope to incorporate or blend these traditions?

_____

_____

_____

_____

_____

_____

_____

Be thankful

209 DATE: _____

What do you think your purpose or calling is in life? What is the passion that drives you and stirs your heart?

_____

_____

_____

_____

_____

_____

210 DATE: _____

Some of us are more open with our expressions of love. Imagine you are writing a public Valentine's Day message about your loved one on social media. What would you want to say about them to your family and friends?

_____

_____

_____

_____

_____

_____

_____

211 DATE: _____

If you were in a play or musical, where would you be listed in the program? Would you be part of the stage crew, the lead actor, the supporting cast, or the director? What special touch would you bring to the production?

_____

_____

_____

_____

_____

_____

_____

212 DATE: _____

What is your best mode of communication? Particularly with a difficult or serious subject, when you want to get it right and be heard clearly, how will you communicate?

_____

_____

_____

_____

_____

_____

_____

213 DATE: _____

What is one trait or quality about your loved one that made you fall in love and know this person was a great fit for you? How do they demonstrate this quality?

_____

_____

_____

_____

_____

_____

214 DATE: _____

Our sense of touch gives us so much information about what is around us. Touch your partner's hand or sleeve. Describe how being close to them makes you feel.

_____

_____

_____

_____

_____

_____

_____

215 DATE: _____

Share a spiritual rite of passage, such as baptism. How did it shape your faith and become a pivotal part of your faith journey?

_____

_____

_____

_____

_____

_____

216 DATE: _____

You are tourists this weekend in a nearby city. Where will you both be exploring? Will you be at the art museum, a concert, a ball game, or somewhere else?

_____

_____

_____

_____

_____

_____

217 DATE: _____

Jesus said to the disciples in Mark 1:17, "Come follow me and I will make you fishers of men." What do you feel he meant for them and for us?

_____

_____

_____

_____

_____

_____

_____

218 DATE: _____

It's wonderful to engage all our senses. What is a favorite scent your loved one wears or uses around the home? What draws you to it?

_____

_____

_____

_____

_____

_____

_____

219 DATE: _____

Ephesians 4:32 says, "Be kind and compassionate to one another, forgiving each other, just as in Christ God forgave you." Who is typically first to apologize and end a disagreement?

_____

_____

_____

_____

_____

_____

PEACE

220 DATE: _____

When it comes to the children in your life—be they your own or those of family and friends—are you a stern guardian or more relaxed? Are the two of you different in your styles?

_____

_____

_____

_____

_____

_____

221 DATE: _____

As you get older, do you feel you have gained a higher tolerance or lower tolerance for other people's baggage or drama? Do you feel time has softened or hardened you?

_____

_____

_____

_____

_____

_____

222 DATE: _____

Famous landmarks span the globe and mark our history. Which landmarks would you most like to see and why? Which areas have you seen already?

_____

_____

_____

_____

_____

_____

223 DATE: _____

1 Peter 4:16 says, "If you suffer as a Christian, do not be ashamed." Have you faced any challenges because of your faith and beliefs? How did you handle that situation?

_____

_____

_____

_____

_____

_____

224 DATE: _____

Blueprints give an architect the future plans for building. Do you feel you have blueprints for your future with your loved one?

_____

_____

_____

_____

_____

_____

225 DATE: _____

1 John 1:1 says, "We saw him with our own eyes." (NLT) If you saw Jesus walking down the street today, what would you like to speak with him about? What would you say?

_____

_____

_____

_____

_____

_____

_____

226 DATE: _____

If you could enhance any feature to your house for the sole purpose of fun, what would you add? For example, a slide instead of stairs, a movie theater, batting cages, or maybe a library.

_____

_____

_____

_____

_____

_____

_____

227 DATE: _____

When it comes to sports, do you prefer to watch or participate (or just leave the room)? What is your best or favorite sport? Of course, please share your favorite teams.

_____

_____

_____

_____

_____

_____

228 DATE: _____

Do you have a celebration ritual in your relationship? Maybe you always give flowers on Valentine's Day or eat cake for your anniversary. If not, what ritual can you start to incorporate?

_____

_____

_____

_____

_____

_____

_____

229 DATE: _____

Sometimes even when surrounded by people, we can feel alone. Are there times or situations where you feel lonely in your relationship? How can the two of you combat that distance?

_____

_____

_____

_____

_____

_____

230 DATE: _____

Write about your most embarrassing moment. Take this moment to laugh together and share comforting words with your partner.

_____

_____

_____

_____

_____

_____ *BE BRAVE*

231 DATE: _____

Psalm 1:1 speaks about the "joys of those who do not follow the advice of the wicked." (NLT) What is the worst advice you have ever gotten? Did you take it?

_____

_____

_____

_____

_____

_____

_____

232 DATE: _____

Imagine you are planning a weekend camping trip together. Will you be camping in the rough or glamping in a comfortable camper? Describe it here.

_____

_____

_____

_____

_____

_____

233 DATE: _____

Consider the children in your life who may ask you the question, "Do our pets go to heaven?" What are your thoughts on this? Will we see our animal friends again one day in heaven?

_____

_____

_____

_____

_____

_____

234 DATE: _____

How would you describe your fashion choices or sense of style? Do you lean toward casual wear or more business-ready? What do you love about your partner's style?

_____

_____

_____

_____

_____

_____

_____

235 DATE: _____

Where do you fall in the birth order of your family: first-born, middle, last, or only child? How do you think that family position affects your personality and life decisions?

_____

_____

_____

_____

_____

_____

236 DATE: _____

Have you ever felt the entrepreneurial spirit and been inspired to start a business venture? What was it? Or what business venture or product would you like to create?

_____

_____

_____

_____

_____

_____

_____

237 DATE: _____

In Luke 8:50 Jesus said to a man with a dying child, "Don't be afraid; just believe, and she will be healed." Have you ever witnessed Christ's healing or even a miracle? Do you believe miracles still happen today?

_____

_____

_____

_____

_____

_____

_____

238 DATE: _____

Intimacy is more than just what happens in the bedroom. How can you foster emotional intimacy in your relationship?

_____

_____

_____

_____

_____

_____

239 DATE: _____

High school leaves an impression on all of us. Set the scene for your partner. What were you like in high school and how are you different now?

_____

_____

_____

_____

_____

_____

_____

240 DATE: _____

Do you tend to handle situations together as a team? Or do you lean toward attending to problems on your own, then coming together and sharing the resolution at the end?

_____

_____

_____

_____

_____

_____

_____

241 DATE: _____

1 John 5:21 says, "Dear children, keep yourselves from idols." Write about something that might need to change priority levels in your heart.

_____

_____

_____

_____

_____

_____

242 DATE: _____

If you were both contestants on a trivia game show, what would be your winning subject or content area? Write a trivia question for your loved one on their favorite topic.

_____

_____

_____

_____

_____

_____

_____

ALWAYS

243 DATE: _____

Knowing about your ancestors helps form your identity. How much have you learned about your family's past or what research have you done? How has it shaped you?

_____

_____

_____

_____

_____

_____

244 DATE: _____

This question is always fun to ask and remember: How did your relationship begin? Which of you invited the other on that first date?

_____

_____

_____

_____

_____

_____

245 DATE: _____

Our jobs can teach us many things, from specific skills to working with others. What have you learned from each of your jobs?

_____

_____

_____

_____

_____

_____

_____

246 DATE: _____

Swimming against the tide is not easy. When have you gone against the tide with a life choice or decision? How did that work out?

_____

_____

_____

_____

_____

_____

_____

 **247** DATE: _____

You each may have different visions of what romance means in a relationship. Describe a romantic evening with your loved one or what you consider to be a romantic gesture.

_____

_____

_____

_____

_____

_____

_____

248 DATE: _____

Reading large sections of the Bible in a year or studying a particular book is a great accomplishment. What kind of faith study has been most meaningful to you and why?

_____

_____

_____

_____

_____

_____

249 DATE: _____

What is a home, personal, or professional skill you would like to learn in the next few years? Write down some steps you can take together to learn this skill.

_____

_____

_____

_____

_____

_____

_____

250 DATE: _____

Matthew 6:8 speaks about prayer, saying, "Your Father knows what you need before you ask him!" If God knows what we need, what do you think is the purpose of prayer?

_____

_____

_____

_____

_____

_____

_____

251 DATE: _____

Imagine you are the author of a mystery novel or screenplay. Plan your plot together and create a detective to solve the case.

_____

_____

_____

_____

_____

_____

_____

252 DATE: _____

People change and grow over time. Do you feel you or your partner have changed and grown over the course of your relationship? How has that enhanced your relationship?

_____

_____

_____

_____

_____

_____

_____

253 DATE: _____

If you were to become famous, what would it be for?
Maybe a famous chef, musician, influencer, or athlete?
What skills and qualities would propel you to stardom?

_____

_____

_____

_____

_____

_____

_____

254 DATE: _____

We can't change the past. But is there a moment in your
life you wish you could revisit? What would you change?

_____

_____

_____

_____

_____

_____

_____

255 DATE:_____

2 John 5 says, "I ask that we love one another." How have you shown love to each other today?

_____

_____

_____

_____

_____

_____

_____

256 DATE:_____

What is the first event of national importance that you remember? What is the most significant event that's happened in your lifetime? How did it affect you?

_____

_____

_____

_____

_____

_____

_____

257 DATE: _____

Imagine the two of you put together a time capsule to be opened 10 years from now. What items would you include?

_____

_____

_____

_____

_____

_____

_____

258 DATE: _____

How can you be the hands and feet of Jesus? In other words, how can you actively and tangibly show God's love to your friends and/or a community in need?

_____

_____

_____

_____

_____

_____

_____

259 DATE: _____

How are the two of you most alike in personality? In what ways are you complete opposites? How can you use these similarities and differences to complement each other?

_____

_____

_____

_____

_____

_____

260 DATE: _____

How do you hope to leave a better world for future generations? What small steps can you take in your everyday life to achieve this?

_____

_____

_____

_____

_____

_____

261 DATE: _____

What do you desire most for yourself and for your relationship in the year to come?

_____

_____

_____

_____

_____

_____

_____

_____

262 DATE: _____

Laughter brings us close, lifts the spirit, feeds the soul, and warms the heart. What have you done together recently that made you both laugh?

_____

_____

_____

_____

_____

_____

263 DATE: _____

We all have quirks that make us unique in our personality. What is one of your quirks? Ask your partner to name one of the quirks they love about you.

_____

_____

_____

_____

_____

_____

_____

264 DATE: _____

Sleep, or lack of it, affects our health. What are your sleep patterns? Are you a light sleeper or a heavy one? Are you a night owl or an early riser?

_____

_____

_____

_____

_____

_____

265 DATE: _____

The Prayer of Jabez in 1 Chronicles 4:10 says, "Bless me and enlarge my territory." What meaning do you take from this verse? How do you wish God to bless and expand your life together as a couple?

_____

_____

_____

_____

_____

_____

266 DATE: _____

What has been your biggest struggle in life—emotional, mental, or another obstacle? How have you sought to overcome it?

_____

_____

_____

_____

_____

_____

267 DATE: _____

Do you have pet names for each other? How did they come about? If you don't have any, write about any nick-names you have from childhood or as an adult.

_____

_____

_____

_____

_____

_____

268 DATE: _____

Have the spiritual rituals of faith and/or church become routine, or are you able to approach them with fresh thought and reflection? How do you keep your heart open to these faith practices?

_____

_____

_____

_____

_____

_____ *Faith*

_____

269 DATE: _____

Adult friendships can be difficult to cultivate. Books have been written on how to build them. How can you reach out to nurture and grow friendships with other adults?

_____

_____

_____

_____

_____

_____

_____

270 DATE: _____

In Ruth 1:16, Ruth says to her mother-in-law, "Where you go, I will go." What relationship would you like to have with your partner's family and how can they help?

_____

_____

_____

_____

_____

_____

_____

271 DATE: _____

Tiny homes have become a niche real estate market. Could you live together in a tiny home? If you already do, how do you like it? Write about the pros and cons.

_____

_____

_____

_____

_____

_____

_____

272 DATE: _____

What do you love to do when you come home and walk in the door? Write about any greetings, rituals, or other things that bring you joy and comfort.

_____

_____

_____

_____

_____

_____

_____

273 DATE: _____

If you could resolve one national or world problem in the next 10 years, what would it be and how would you start?

_____

_____

_____

_____

_____

_____

_____

274 DATE: _____

If you were asked to substitute teach at your local school, what grade and/or subject would be your best fit? Describe how you think the day would go.

_____

_____

_____

_____

_____

_____

_____

275 DATE: _____

You're stranded on a deserted island with a five-gallon jug of water and a few days' worth of food. What other three things would you hope to have, and why?

_____

_____

_____

_____

_____

_____

276 DATE: _____

In Psalm 95:2 David writes about worship, saying, "Let us sing psalms of praise to him." (NLT) What is your favorite worship song? Why is it meaningful or what memories does it hold for you?

_____

_____

_____

_____

_____

_____

277 DATE: _____

Do you make decisions easily or do you tend to sit on them for a bit? What helps you with your decision-making process and can you work together to improve?

_____

_____

_____

_____

_____

_____

_____

278 DATE: _____

In what ways does technology improve or hinder your relationship? If you put aside technology for a set amount of time each week, what do you think would happen between you?

_____

_____

_____

_____

_____

_____

_____

279 DATE: _____

Song of Solomon 2:2 describes their beloved as, "Like a lily among thorns is my darling among the young women." Use similar romantic language to describe your loved one.

_____

_____

_____

_____

_____

_____

_____

280 DATE: _____

As you grow in your relationship and love, you are building a shared history. Whether you have been together five months or fifteen years, what is your favorite memory so far?

_____

_____

_____

_____

_____

_____

281 DATE: _____

Our lifestyles thrive on busyness. If you could hire out or automate any part of your day, what would it be and why?

_____

_____

_____

_____

_____

_____

_____

282 DATE: _____

Titus 3:5 says, "He saved us, not because of righteous things we had done, but because of his mercy." What does it mean to be saved by grace?

_____

_____

_____

_____

_____

_____

MERCY

283 DATE: _____

When it comes to cheering for sports, are you a house divided or do you support the same team? When it's game time, how do you make competition fun?

_____

_____

_____

_____

_____

_____

284 DATE: _____

Earlier in this journal, you were awarded an imaginary inheritance. But have you ever won something real? Perhaps the lottery or a raffle, maybe the school spelling bee? Share and celebrate.

_____

_____

_____

_____

_____

_____

285 DATE: _____

If you travel for business or are apart for whatever reason, how do you stay connected with each other? In what ways can you plan to stay close when you are apart?

_____

_____

_____

_____

_____

_____ TRUST

_____

286 DATE: _____

Have you seen God answer prayers in your life or the lives of those around you? Share how He has responded and its impact on your spiritual life.

_____

_____

_____

_____

_____

_____

287 DATE: _____

Do you have many photos together or are you a little camera shy? Do you prefer professional or candid shots? How do you capture your memories?

_____

_____

_____

_____

_____

_____

_____

288 DATE: _____

Are you a social butterfly? How much do you enjoy or expect to be out with others? If your response is different from your partner's, how do you find balance?

_____

_____

_____

_____

_____

_____

_____

289 DATE: _____

Share a financial goal the two of you have made for the future. Maybe it's to correct a past mistake, establish good stewardship, or learn more about a certain field of finance.

_____

_____

_____

_____

_____

_____

290 DATE: _____

What is your phone conversation style? Do you enjoy a long phone chat with family and friends? Perhaps you prefer a quick catch-up call or text messages. Are you two similar? How does this play out in your relationship?

_____

_____

_____

_____

_____

_____

291 DATE: _____

We all love to snuggle up together on the sofa with a great story to watch on TV. What television series or movies do the two of you binge-watch together?

_____

_____

_____

_____

_____

_____

292 DATE: _____

At the holidays, do you go all out with home decorations and holiday-themed clothing? Or do you prefer a low-key celebration with subtle or no displays? How do you balance each other?

_____

_____

_____

_____

_____

_____

293 DATE: _____

John 10:27 says, "My sheep listen to my voice; I know them." How can you know that you are hearing God's voice? What can you do to work on listening?

_____

_____

_____

_____

_____

_____

_____

294 DATE: _____

Do you like to invest in the stock market? If you could buy shares of any company, which would it be and why would you like to support it?

_____

_____

_____

_____

_____

_____

295 DATE: _____

How comfortable are you with public displays of affection? Do you enjoy holding hands, maybe even a kiss, or do you prefer to keep affectionate displays for private time?

_____

_____

_____

_____

_____

_____

296 DATE: _____

Have you ever won an award? Describe your accomplishment. If you haven't, what would you wish to win an award for? Who would you thank in your acceptance speech?

_____

_____

_____

_____

_____

_____

_____

297 DATE: _____

If you ever were to grow complacent or fall away from the faith, what steps would you take to answer your questions and concerns or strengthen your relationship with God?

_____

_____

_____

_____

_____

_____

298 DATE: _____

Being in a relationship means getting older together. How do you see your relationship growing as you age?

_____

_____

_____

_____

_____

_____

Joyful

299 DATE: _____

When you were single, did you ever have the opportunity to travel alone? What do you love most about travel now that you can go on trips as a couple?

_____

_____

_____

_____

_____

_____

300 DATE: _____

Easter and Christmas have great value and importance in our faith. What other religious holidays are important for you and how do you observe them?

_____

_____

_____

_____

_____

_____

301 DATE: _____

How many languages can you speak? What language would you like to learn if you had the time, and how would you like to use it?

_____

_____

_____

_____

_____

_____

_____

302 DATE: _____

Matthew 18:20 encourages us, "For where two or three gather in my name, there am I with them." What has either hindered or motivated you to gather with other believers?

_____

_____

_____

_____

_____

_____

303 DATE: _____

How do you handle potentially awkward social situations such as riding an elevator with a stranger? How do you break the silence? How do you feel? Do you have any funny stories to share?

_____

_____

_____

_____

_____

_____

_____

304 DATE: _____

Think about someone who passed away who was very special to you. Share a special memory with your partner about that person and how they touched your life.

_____

_____

_____

_____

_____

_____

305 DATE: _____

What happens when a conflict cannot be resolved in the moment? It takes work to move to a place where you can amicably agree to disagree. How can you move toward peace in the future when you don't see eye to eye?

_____

_____

_____

_____

_____

_____

306 DATE: _____

Song of Solomon 2:16 says, "My beloved is mine and I am his." How do you know when you have found true love? How does your heart identify the real deal?

_____

_____

_____

_____

_____

_____ *Grateful*

307 DATE: _____

When it comes to outdoor activities, do you prefer to be in the water or on dry land? Write about any activities you like doing together and what you enjoy about them.

_____

_____

_____

_____

_____

_____

308 DATE: _____

Are you a good listener? Each of you share one funny or positive moment from your day. Maintain eye contact with each other while speaking and listening. Record your thoughts below.

_____

_____

_____

_____

_____

_____   LOVE

_____

309 DATE: _____

Bucket lists are dreams we hope to accomplish in the future. We often make an individual list, but do you have a bucket list as a couple? What would you dream together?

_____

_____

_____

_____

_____

_____

_____

310 DATE: _____

How are you most like your parents, family, or those who helped raise you? Do you share any beloved qualities? Sometimes we pick up subtle traits that a partner may pinpoint better than we do!

_____

_____

_____

_____

_____

_____

♥ 311 DATE: _____

Do you think your name fits you? Imagine you have the opportunity to change your name or use a pen name. What would be your new name and why would it suit you?

_____

_____

_____

_____

_____

_____

◀ 312 DATE: _____

What musical instrument do you play or wish you could learn? What do you love about this instrument? If you play, how long have you played and was it difficult to master?

_____

_____

_____

_____

_____

_____

_____

313 DATE: _____

The Thanksgiving holiday is typically steeped in family traditions. What Thanksgiving traditions do you have with your family and what traditions have you started together as a couple?

_____

_____

_____

_____

_____

_____

314 DATE: _____

What do you think is more important, to be right or to be at peace? When you disagree with someone, or each other, in the end does being right or at peace have higher value?

_____

_____

_____

_____

_____

Peace

315 DATE: _____

Do you have a song that you have adopted for your relationship? Or what song do you feel fits your relationship best? Why do you believe this song speaks to your relationship?

_____

_____

_____

_____

_____

_____

316 DATE: _____

As a child, did your family have a favorite spot for outings or vacations? Share your favorite spot and a happy memory of those outings or trips.

_____

_____

_____

_____

_____

_____

 **317** DATE: _____

Hebrews 13:16 says, "Don't forget to do good and to
share with those in need." Have you participated in a
mission or service project? Is this something you hope
to do together?

_____

_____

_____

_____

_____

_____

_____

318 DATE: _____

What are you most sentimental about? What really
touches your heart and moves you to feel emotional?
Is it a past memory, a sensitive commercial, or maybe a
certain object that triggers a memory?

_____

_____

_____

_____

_____

_____

♥ 319 DATE: _____

Describe your ideal breakfast routine. Do you have a favorite meal, beverage, or way to start the day? What morning preferences do you share?

_____

_____

_____

_____

_____

_____

_____

◀ 320 DATE: _____

Has it been a challenge to divide and balance the household tasks with your relationship? What needs to be adjusted to make more space for couple time?

_____

_____

_____

_____

_____

_____

_____

321 DATE: _____

Psalm 139:17 speaks to God's love for us: "How precious to me are your thoughts." How important is self-love and self-acceptance to the health of your relationship as a couple?

_____

_____

_____

_____

_____

_____

322 DATE: _____

A family member or friend decides to make a surprise visit. Do you enjoy spur-of-the moment visits or do you need advance notice from guests? Do you and your partner have different opinions on this issue?

_____

_____

_____

_____

_____

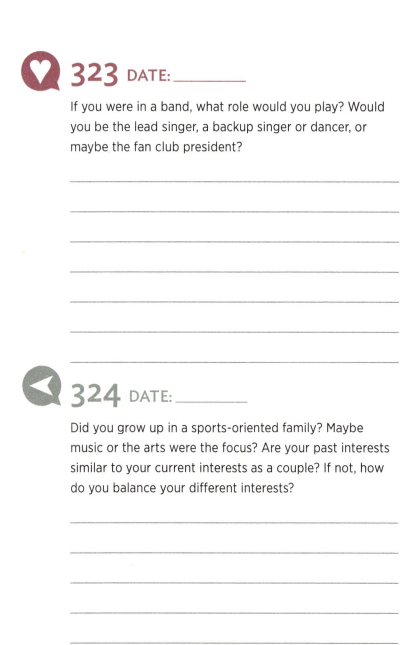

323 DATE: _____

If you were in a band, what role would you play? Would you be the lead singer, a backup singer or dancer, or maybe the fan club president?

_____

_____

_____

_____

_____

_____

324 DATE: _____

Did you grow up in a sports-oriented family? Maybe music or the arts were the focus? Are your past interests similar to your current interests as a couple? If not, how do you balance your different interests?

_____

_____

_____

_____

_____

_____

PRAISE

325 DATE: _____

Philippians 4:19 promises, "This same God who takes care of me will supply all your needs." (NLT) In hard times, how can you rely on God for wisdom and support?

_____

_____

_____

_____

_____

_____ Faith

_____

326 DATE: _____

If you go for a drive or a walk to clear your mind or just be quiet together, where do you go? What is your route with no real errand in mind?

_____

_____

_____

_____

_____

_____

_____

327 DATE: _____

Romans 12:9 says, "Love must be sincere." Do you show genuine love for your partner? How do you display your love for each other?

_____

_____

_____

_____

_____

_____

_____

328 DATE: _____

Respect for each other is a key component to lasting relationships. How do you show respect to each other through your actions and speech?

_____

_____

_____

_____

_____

_____

_____

329 DATE: _____

Although we make every effort, our priorities as a couple may not always be in sync. How can you work to continue to support each other when your priorities do not align?

_____

_____

_____

_____

_____

_____

330 DATE: _____

Do you ever feel conflicted with secular media when it clashes with your Christian values? How do you respond?

_____

_____

_____

_____

_____

_____

_____ *Self-control*

331 DATE: _____

As a couple, you are a team. There are the two of you, and God, working in union. When is the last time you worked as a team and had each other's back?

_____

_____

_____

_____

_____

_____

332 DATE: _____

Proverbs 13:20 says, "Walk with the wise and become wise." How does your community and choice of friendships influence your relationship and faith?

_____

_____

_____

_____

_____

_____

_____

333 DATE: _____

Ephesians 4:29 says, "Do not let any unwholesome talk come out of your mouths, but only what is helpful." What goals can you set for taming the tongue and speaking words that uplift?

_____

_____

_____

_____

_____

_____

_____

Stay
STRONG

334 DATE: _____

We each come from unique family, cultural, faith, and economic backgrounds. How have those differences enhanced your relationship? What have you learned from each other?

_____

_____

_____

_____

_____

335 DATE: _____

We all have an occasional bad day or receive disappointing news. What cheers you up and why? What has your partner done recently that brightened your hard day?

_____

_____

_____

_____

_____

_____

_____

336 DATE: _____

Colossians 3:14 says, "Put on love, which binds them all together in perfect unity." What do you feel is a unique strength of your relationship that binds you as a team?

_____

_____

_____

_____

_____

_____

_____

337 DATE: _____

The Christmas season can be a hectic time of year. How can you be proactive in keeping the focus on the birth of Christ as the reason for the celebration?

_____

_____

_____

_____

_____

_____

338 DATE: _____

We may be at different points in our spiritual faith, but prayer is always something we can do together. Write down and share a prayer request for today with your loved one.

_____

_____

_____

_____

_____

_____

pray

339 DATE: _____

If you were a cartoon character, who would it be? What qualities about that character best fit you?

_____

_____

_____

_____

_____

_____

340 DATE: _____

What is your favorite part of the day and why? Is it your morning coffee, a productive afternoon, or maybe an evening at home? What's the best part of your day together?

_____

_____

_____

_____

_____

_____

_____

> **341** DATE: _____

What does your ideal relationship together look like 20 years from now? How can you work to improve and grow toward this place?

_____

_____

_____

_____

_____

_____

342 DATE: _____

Romans 12:15 speaks to caring for others: "Rejoice with those who rejoice; mourn with those who mourn." How can you learn to be empathetic for your community?

_____

_____

_____

_____

_____

_____

_____

343 DATE: _____

Do you collect anything? Maybe you have a coin collection, vintage records, or perhaps you collect journals or books. What do you treasure and what inspired you to start your collection?

_____

_____

_____

_____

_____

_____

_____

344 DATE: _____

How much time do you spend socializing with friends and family? Is this a comfortable fit for you and your relationship? Would you prefer more or less time?

_____

_____

_____

_____

_____

_____

_____

345 DATE: _____

If there comes a time when a child in your life goes down a path you do not agree with, how will you keep sight of your love for them while encouraging and comforting each other as a couple?

_____

_____

_____

_____

_____

_____

346 DATE: _____

In Acts 20:7, Paul recounts, "On the first day of the week we came together to break bread." What does the act of communion mean to you?

_____

_____

_____

_____

_____

_____

_____

347 DATE: _____

Imagine you run to pick up your partner's favorite foods around town. What are they and where did you get them? Compare notes; did you guess correctly?

_____

_____

_____

_____

_____

_____

348 DATE: _____

What Christmas music, movies, programs, or other holiday entertainment do you enjoy? Are there any special meals you love to eat during the season?

_____

_____

_____

_____

_____

_____

rejoice

349 DATE: _____

Is there one thing you want to accomplish in your lifetime? Have you achieved it yet? How do you plan to capture that ambition, and are you on the way?

_____

_____

_____

_____

_____

_____

_____

350 DATE: _____

Have you ever kept a prayer journal? Use this space to write down your prayer requests or those of friends, and return later to document God's answer to those prayers.

_____

_____

_____

_____

_____

_____

_____

351 DATE: _____

If you could swap lives with anyone for 24 hours, who would you choose? Why did this person come to mind?

_____

_____

_____

_____

_____

_____

352 DATE: _____

In your younger days, did you ever go to camp, a church retreat, a sleepover, or anywhere on your own? What are your best memories?

_____

_____

_____

_____

_____

_____

_____

_____

353 DATE: _____

Do you have a book that you have not read but feel you should? What makes you think this particular book should be on your must-read list?

_____

_____

_____

_____

_____

_____

_____

354 DATE: _____

Matthew 16:26 says, "What good will it be for someone to gain the whole world, yet forfeit their soul?" When making decisions together, how do you consider the effect on your faith?

_____

_____

_____

_____

_____

_____

_____

355 DATE: _____

If you could be a guest star on any TV show or podcast, where would you be featured? Why this show? Would you be cast together?

_____

_____

_____

_____

_____

_____

356 DATE: _____

We've covered a lot of ground in this journal! But what is one topic you wish you and your partner could talk about, or talk about more often, and why?

_____

_____

_____

_____

_____

_____

357 DATE: _____

What three things would you like to do before the end of the year? Either as a couple or cheering each other on, write personal or professional year-end goals. Are there any steps you can take toward doing these things?

_____

_____

_____

_____

_____

_____

358 DATE: _____

Imagine you are going to give a talk to a large group of people to pass on your knowledge about a particular topic. What would your subject matter be and what would you want to say?

_____

_____

_____

_____

_____

_____

_____

359 DATE: _____

Spicy, saucy, tangy, or salty—what do your taste buds crave? What is a condiment that you just cannot live without? Is there a condiment you cannot tolerate?

_____

_____

_____

_____

_____

_____

360 DATE: _____

If you were the president or leader of a nation, how would you respond to current events? Are there other wise leaders you would seek out for counsel?

_____

_____

_____

_____

_____

_____

_____

361 DATE: _____

Matthew 7:1 warns, "Do not judge, or you too will be judged." It's easy to leap to judgment, but how can you learn to show love and understanding instead?

_____

_____

_____

_____

_____

_____

362 DATE: _____

Write about an event that most shaped the person you have become or at least the person you would like to be. Share and discuss with your partner.

_____

_____

_____

_____

_____

_____

363 DATE:_____

Just like a sports team, if your relationship had a mascot, what would it be? Get creative! You can even draw a picture of your mascot.

_____

_____

_____

_____

_____

_____

364 DATE:_____

Romans 10:13 says, "For everyone who calls on the name of the Lord will be saved." Share with your loved one how you came to be a Christian.

_____

_____

_____

_____

_____

_____

_____

 **365** DATE:＿＿＿＿＿

You have reached your final question together—what an accomplishment! What have you learned about each other and how did you grow in your relationship during this yearlong journey?

_____

_____

_____

_____

_____

_____

_____

Grow as a Couple with God by Your Side

CONGRATULATIONS on completing this yearlong journey together! I am so proud of the commitment you made to your relationship and to growing in your faith. Exploring these topics through writing in this journal and talking things over together has brought you closer as a couple— and I hope you had fun along the way.

You can continue this momentum by setting aside a few minutes every day for conversation, fun, and meaningful discussion that deepens your knowledge of each other. I encourage you to pray for each other. Grow your faith by reading a daily passage of scripture together. I hope this journal has enriched your relationship and your faith.

ACKNOWLEDGMENTS

TO ADRIAN and the Callisto Media team, thank you for your support on this fun project. To the Joyful Stepmom community, your friendship is treasured. To our parents, thank you for setting a wonderful example. Stephen, I am reminded with joy of your childhood. Matt, love you! I'm looking forward to a lifetime of conversations.

ABOUT THE AUTHOR

 EMILY JORDAN is the author of *The Blended Family Devotional for Couples* and founder of The Joyful Stepmom, a Christian ministry. The ministry includes an online community, a website, and local chapters. She is a contributing writer and invited speaker for marriage and blended family support. Emily and Matt were married in 2005 and live in the Midwest with their little watchdog, Buster. She is the proud stepmom of a kind young man.